All Kinds of Bees

Bees have been on earth for more than fifty million years. Today, in many varied forms, there are more of them than ever before.

Dorothy Shuttlesworth describes the different families of bees and the ways in which they live. You will find out about bees that live in colonies and bees that live alone; bees that build and bees that tunnel; bees that work for man and, even, bees that work against him. All kinds of bees.

ALL KINDS OF BEES

BY

Dorothy E. Shuttlesworth

ILLUSTRATED BY

Su Zan Noguchi Swain

RANDOM HOUSE   NEW YORK

This title was originally cataloged by the Library of Congress as follows:
Shuttlesworth, Dorothy Edwards, 1907–
All kinds of bees, by Dorothy E. Shuttlesworth. Illustrated by
Su Zan Noguchi Swain. New York, Random House [1967]
62 p.   illus.   24 cm.   (Gateway books)
1. Bees—Juvenile literature.   i. Swain, Su Zan (Noguchi) illus.   ii. Title.
PZ10.S65A1   j 595.79   67–9156
ISBN: 0-394-80143-1   0-394-90143-6 (lib. bdg.)

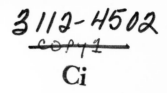
For Lynn
who is a 'honey'

Contents

All Kinds of Bees

Honeybee with full pollen basket

I
The Parts of a Bee

There are all kinds of bees. Big bees, tiny bees. Bees that live in colonies. Bees that live alone. Bees that sting. Bees that do not sting. With so many kinds of bees you may wonder: What features are shared by *all* members of this group of insects?

One important part of any bee is its long proboscis or tongue. The tip is spoonlike, and, behind it, the underside of the proboscis is rounded into a tube. Through this the bee sucks water, nectar from flowers, and mud that is sometimes used for building.

The body hairs of a bee are feathery. They are well suited for entangling and holding pollen grains. And special pollen-holding hairs make pollen-carrying baskets on the legs or body.

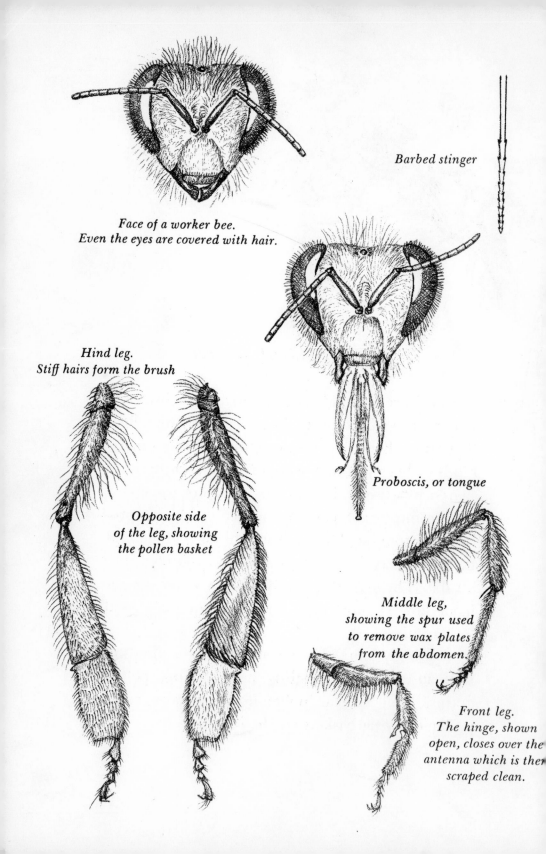

Barbed stinger

Face of a worker bee.
Even the eyes are covered with hair.

Hind leg.
Stiff hairs form the brush

Opposite side
of the leg, showing
the pollen basket

Proboscis, or tongue

Middle leg,
showing the spur used
to remove wax plates
from the abdomen.

Front leg.
The hinge, shown
open, closes over the
antenna which is then
scraped clean.

opening for breathing
(hair removed)

front wing

HEAD

hind wing

compound eye

antenna

THORAX

ABDOMEN

stinger

front leg

middle leg

hind leg

Because they depend on flowers, a keen sense of smell is important to bees. The fragrance of a flower helps guide them to nectar. They can also detect by smell whether another bee approaching the nest belongs there or to another colony. But a bee does not have a nose. Its openings for breathing are on its body, not on its head. They play no part in detecting smells. A bee "smells" with its antennae, or feelers. Nerve fibers connect the sensitive feelers with the brain. They tell the bee what lies near.

When a bee touches something with her feelers, she receives still more information. She can feel the shape of the object. The feelers are of

5

great importance inside the hive too. They help the bee to do various kinds of work there. A bee whose antennae have been injured or lost is quite helpless.

Apparently bees are not able to hear. No type of ear has ever been discovered on them, and they do not react to sound in any way. Of course if someone knocks against a beehive, the bees are disturbed. But this is because they feel their home being shaken, not because they hear anything.

Though they lack ears, bees are well supplied with eyes. Like a number of other insects, they have two large eyes with three tiny eyes set between them. Each of the large eyes rises from one side of the head. It is made up of many thousands

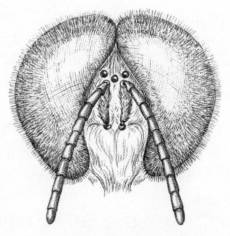

Head of a drone
The compound eyes are made up of many tiny cones

of neat little cones packed tightly together. This is a "compound" eye. The bee cannot roll her eyes or focus them. But as she flies, she becomes aware of what lies around and below her, and she can recognize many outlines. She can also recognize color, although not always in the way human eyes do. Bees see only four colors clearly — blue, blue-green, yellow and ultra-violet. Many flowers reflect ultra-violet light, which is invisible to the human eye. Bees also recognize flowers by their size and shape.

The mandibles, or jaws, of a bee are of great service as working tools. They are located on each side of the mouth. They move sideways rather than up and down.

The secret of a bee's success in collecting nectar for the benefit of her colony is her double stomach. When she swallows nectar, it does not go into a true stomach but to a storage compartment. This is called the honey stomach. As soon as a worker returns to her hive, the nectar is brought up again, or regurgitated, to be fed to the young bees. Or the worker may store it in cells. But when she is hungry, a valve opens between the honey stomach and the true stomach allowing some honey to run in. Only then is it digested.

A bee does not swallow the pollen she collects. She molds it into a solid mass, moistening some

of it with nectar, and attaches it to her pollen
baskets. As she flies home, she may look as if she
is wearing tiny, baggy pants.

Wings and legs grow from the thorax or middle section of the bee. There are four wings, but
the front and hind wing are so close together they
seem to be only one.

Behind the thorax is the hind-body, or abdomen, and at the tail end of the abdomen is the
stinger.

People are often confused about insect stings.
They are sure that all bees and wasps — and mos-
quitoes, too — die after using their stingers.

A mosquito does not have a stinger. It bites so
that it can feed on the blood of its victim. But
the stinger of bee or wasp is used strictly as a
weapon. Only the females have stingers.

8

At the base of a stinger is a small sac of poison. At its point are little barbs which turn backward. When the bee thrusts her stinger into a victim, the barb holds so firmly she cannot easily pull it out again. As she tears herself away, she leaves part of her internal organs attached to the stinger. Soon she dies. If she were able to pull out the stinger slowly, with a twisting movement, she would not be harmed.

The stingers of queen bees are smooth and can be used over and over. However, they sting only rival queens — not people.

II
The Ways of a Bee

Were you ever stung by a bee? If so, you may have no great liking for bees.

Do you enjoy the taste of rich, golden honey? If so, you may feel that bees are really helpful friends because without them there would be no honey.

Bees *are* helpful, and not only because they make honey. The wax they make is used for floor wax, polishes, cold cream, electrical insulation, candles and colored pencils.

Still more important, bees carry pollen from flower to flower. Because of them, seeds can develop. Without them, many crops of fruits and vegetables, as well as the grasses that feed farm animals, would die away.

Most people know these facts: they know that bees can sting, that they produce honey and wax and that they are helpful to plants. But many do not know that these facts are not true of all bees. There are many "stingless" bees. There are many kinds that do not produce much honey. And there are some that give no special aid to plant life.

People may also say, "Bees live in colonies." Honeybees and some other kinds do — in trees, on the ground or in man-made hives. But not all bees. With many kinds, each bee lives by itself in a solitary shelter.

The bees most easily recognized are the large, fat, yellow and black bumblebees. Yet not all bumblebees fit this description. And there are other families of bees whose members are different in size, color, shape and habits from the bumblebees and from each other. About ten thousand different kinds of bees are to be found in the world.

Does this sound like a tremendous jumble? It could be. But as in a jigsaw puzzle, each of many different parts, or kinds, fits into a pattern that gives us a clear picture.

To begin with, all kinds of bees may be divided into two groups — the social bees, such as the honeybees, and the solitary bees, such as the carpenter bees. There are family groups and divisions within the families, as you will find on page 57.

One other way of grouping bees is by the length and shape of the tongue. The first type of tongue is short and pointed. The second is short and forked. The third is long and ribbonlike. The size and shape of the tongue influences the kinds of flower a bee visits to obtain nectar.

Bees have been living on the earth for a very long time, perhaps fifty times as long as man. There is no evidence that they were here when dinosaurs were living, but by the time mammals were established, bees were on earth too. Fossil remains of some that lived about fifty million years ago have been discovered.

One species — the honeybee — long ago became very important to many people. Let us look first at this kind of bee, and at what goes on in a honeybee hive.

Bees were on earth long before man. This probable ancestor of the modern bee left its shape impressed in a piece of amber. In the drawing, it is shown larger than its true size.

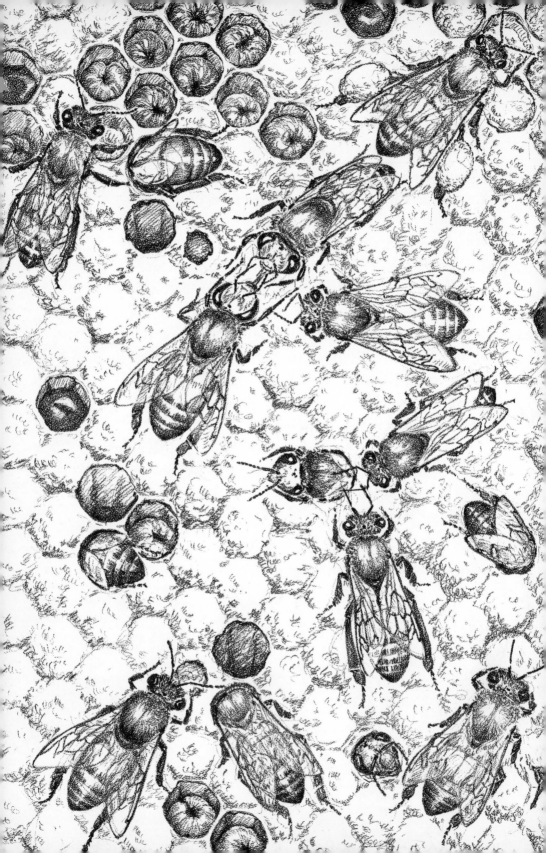

III
Honey Makers

"Long live the queen!"

If honeybees could have a slogan, this might well be it, for a queen is all-important to a colony. It would have no future without her.

Of course other members of a colony are necessary also. Every colony must have drones and workers. But there are hundreds of drones and thousands of workers. There is only one queen.

You probably will never see a queen bee — unless you become a beekeeper and watch carefully over the hives. A queen spends nearly all of her life in the dark interior. Her flights into the sunlit outer world are few and very brief.

She takes her first flight soon after she has reached full growth. And during her first flight, she finds her mate.

Storage cells in a comb. Some hold honey or pollen, others contain young bees. Newly-hatched adults can be seen crawling out of their cells. Their older hive-mates are busy cleaning out cells, packing them with pollen, feeding young bees and passing nectar from mouth to mouth.

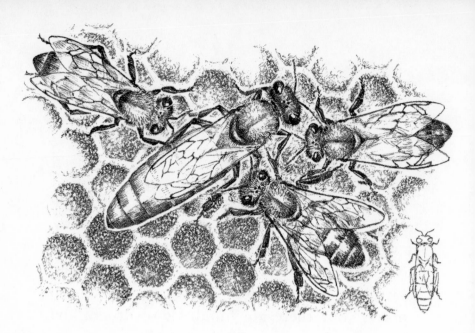

Queen (actual size)

Three workers attending a queen

The young queen circles high into the air followed by a swarm of males — the drones. One of these outdistances the others to reach her. After the mating she returns to the hive to begin laying her eggs — hundreds and hundreds of them every day. They are placed in wax cells called brood cells. As the eggs hatch, the swarm increases rapidly. Within a few weeks it may have as many as thirty thousand members!

When a hive becomes crowded, the queen may take another flight. This time she is not in search of a mate. She is looking for a new home. With her go many workers and some drones. An excited swarm of bees flies from the hive. They circle higher and higher. Finally they come to rest on a convenient perch such as a tree branch. Scouts then begin to look for a new home site. When one is selected, the swarm moves into it. The queen continues her egg-laying and the workers carry on their many duties.

Despite her high-sounding title, the queen bee is not a ruler in any way. She does not guide or direct the workers. In fact, for the most part, she leads a humdrum life. The only occasions on which she uses her wings are when she takes the mating flight or goes in search of a new home.

Still, there is drama in the making of a new queen. Her creation begins with special treatment given to certain eggs or young larvae. The special eggs are placed in roomy, thimble-shaped cells. Unlike the smaller cells for workers and drones, these are not a part of the regular comb. They are the queen cells.

One drone is fed by a worker while another waits its turn

Worker and drone (actual size)

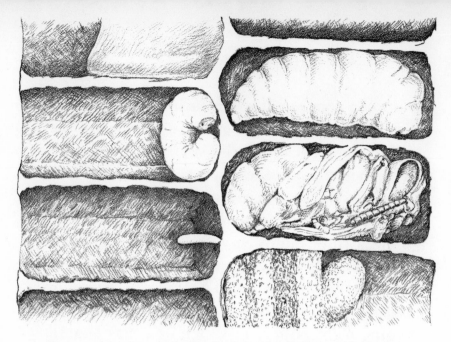

Cross section of a comb. On the left side, the top cell contains honey, the middle cell a young larva and the bottom cell an egg. On the right, the cells, from top to bottom, hold a fully grown larva, a pupa, and layers of packed pollen.

About three days after being laid, all the eggs become fat little grubs — larvae. They are fed by the workers with royal jelly, a substance that comes from the mouths of the workers. It is given to all the larvae. But after two days, the grubs that are to become workers and drones are given a mixture of honey and pollen, called bee-bread. Only the future queens in their special cells are still given royal jelly.

In less than a week the larvae are ready to change to a pupal stage. Each one spins a cocoon of silk, and within this soft wrapping it grows into an adult bee. The drones are ready to chew their way out of their cells after about two weeks

18

as pupae. The workers do so after only twelve days. The young queens are ready to emerge in only seven and a half days.

Usually the old queen leaves her colony just before the new generation emerges. Which of the newcomers will take her place? There can be only one queen to a hive. The first one to come out of her cell becomes the new queen. She is likely to do away with all possible rivals by going to every remaining queen cell and thrusting her stinger into it, killing the occupant. If several young queens happen to break out of their cells at the same time, there is a fight to the death among them. Afterwards the victorious one hurries to kill any other queen-in-the-making before it can emerge. Soon, she leaves on her mating flight.

Queen cells. One has been opened by the emerging queen.

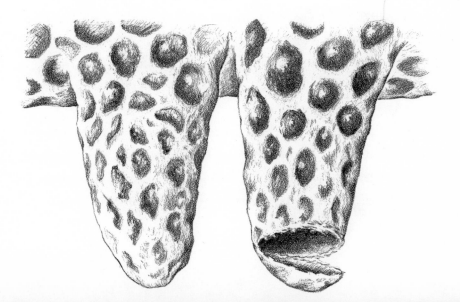

Sometimes the first young queen to emerge may not kill her royal sisters. Then worker bees do away with any extra queen. However, they do not sting her to death. They crush her by "balling." This means that they surround her in a mass of living bodies and squeeze her to death.

While the new queen bee is busy egg-laying, the newly hatched workers have a variety of important jobs. When only two or three days old a worker becomes a nursemaid, tending and feeding the infants and cleaning the hive. The feeding is an enormous task. Each nursemaid makes from two to three thousand trips to a nursery cell before a young one is on its own.

Workers are ready to graduate to new duties when they are about two weeks old. They begin to build cells. By that time wax glands on the underside of the body are fully developed. A

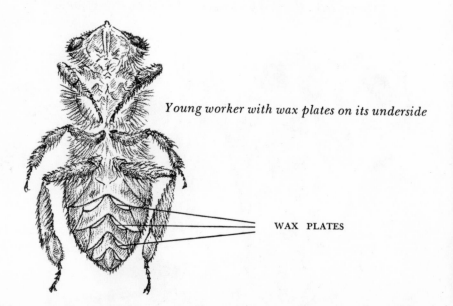

Young worker with wax plates on its underside

WAX PLATES

number of workers of the same age group cling together, and some hold onto the top of the hive. They form a fuzzy curtain. Wax begins to ooze from their wax glands and is pushed up to the mouths and chewed. There it mixes with a fluid that helps to soften it and make it ready for building. Then the workers build the comb.

The comb is a wonderful structure made up of six-sided cells. The cells at the top and sides are for holding honey. Those at the center and bottom are nursery or brood cells for eggs and young.

Any crack or rough spot in the comb is carefully filled in or smoothed over with propolis, or bee glue. This is a sticky substance which worker bees obtain from the buds of plants, especially trees.

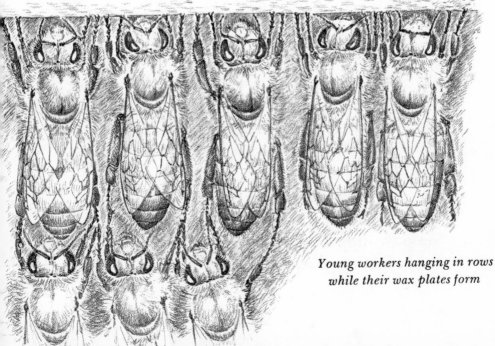

Young workers hanging in rows while their wax plates form

Workers on guard

When the building is completed, the workers have new tasks. Some guard the hive; they stay close to it and defend it from enemies. Many workers devote themselves to housekeeping. They clean out empty brood cells so that the queen can use them again. They carry the bodies of any dead bees away from the hive. In hot weather they cool the hive by fanning the air with their wings.

The workers' last duty is to search out flowers and bring nectar and pollen back to the hive. Pollen serves as food just as it is found. The nectar, however, goes through changes within the bee's body so that it becomes honey. When each worker returns to the hive, a younger worker collects the honey from her. For several minutes the young one sucks it over her tongue, then puts it drop by drop into a storage cell.

At first the honey is quite a thin liquid, but as

22

moisture evaporates, it gradually changes into a heavy syrup. Then the bee seals off the honey cell with wax.

Life among the flowers does not last very long for a honeybee worker. She has already given much of her strength to work within the hive. After several weeks of foraging and collecting, her energy is spent. She dies, and her work is carried on by members of the next generation.

Not all the bees of a colony die with the end of summer. Some of those that emerge in late summer live quietly through the winter. It is their lot to bring the colony alive in the spring. A queen may live for four or five years.

Bees pollinize strawberry plants as they search for pollen

IV
The Bee Dance

As a rule the bees working outside a hive are well organized. There is no helter-skelter flying about to see what they can find. Some act as scouts, looking for supplies of nectar and pollen. Some collect the nectar. Others gather only pollen.

All this organized activity is remarkable. But there is another part of their hunting that is even stranger. This is the bee dance by which a worker informs her hive-mates where food is to be found.

There are two kinds of dances — a round dance and a wagging dance.

The round dance is fairly simple. It is performed when food is less than a hundred yards away from the hive. The worker who has found the food, or the scout, deposits her load of pollen or nectar, then whirls madly around in small circles, first in one direction, then the other. The bees close to her become very excited. In a very

25

short time — a minute or less — she stops dancing and rushes to the door of the hive. Then she flies once more to the place where she discovered the food. No other bee follows her directly, but soon a group of her hive-mates appear at the feeding place.

The wagging dance is more complicated. It gives directions for greater distances. The dancer may first make a short, straight run across the comb or on the platform at the entrance to the hive. As she runs, she wags her abdomen rapidly. Then for several minutes she does a circling dance — to the right, to the left, to the right again — forming a figure 8.

The direction taken by the bee as she makes the straight run shows the direction in which foragers should go. This may be either straight

Round dance

Wagging dance

toward the sun, away from the sun, or at an angle to the right or to the left of the sun. The length of the lines between the two loops of the figure 8 gives a clue as to how far they must fly.

Most of the bees that are alerted by a wagging dance go straight to the good hunting grounds. A few may straggle off independently.

Scientists were puzzled for a long time about bee dances. After they had watched the same kind of performance over and over again, some made guesses as to what it might mean. A few guessed correctly that the dances were a "language" although this explanation seemed incredible. However, careful experiments finally proved without a doubt that the dances are a means of reporting where honey is to be found.

Bees dance also when a swarm is searching for

Bees swarming

a new home. The members of a colony gather around their queen as she rests on a tree branch or other perch. Then dozens of scouts set off in all directions to find a suitable place for a hive such as a hollow tree, a cave or an empty man-made hive.

When a scout discovers a likely nesting place, she returns to her swarm and begins a lively dance right on top of the massed bodies. The better the nesting site, the more excited is her dance. Other successful scouts may return, each beginning a dance of her own. As the attention of other bees is aroused, the swarm splits up. Each group follows a different scout to look at her selection.

When they return, the competition goes on for a while between the rival scouts. Each one tries to persuade the whole swarm to follow her. Finally the entire swarm chooses one scout and flies off with her to the site she has discovered. There they build their new hive and settle in.

No one is sure where the first bees were domesticated. There have been beekeepers in Europe, Africa and Asia for thousands of years, and crossbreeding has helped to make the insects into reliable honey-producing machines. When early colonists came to North America, they brought with them honeybees which the Indians called "the white man's fly."

Beekeepers have learned to save the bees' time and energy. Wax from old combs is melted down. Any impurities are taken out. Then it is rolled out by machines to a proper thickness. The bees need only soften the wax and pull it into shape before they start to store honey.

The beekeeper suspends the comb from the upper part of the hive. Later he may attach it at the sides and bottom. When the bees have filled it, and have had enough honey for their own needs, he can easily remove it. Then he puts the honey into jars and sells it. Beekeeping for honey and wax has become an important industry, especially in the United States, Canada and Australia.

actual size

Bumblebee queen gathering pollen from pussy willows in early spring

V
Bumblebees

Bumblebees are known also as humblebees, but there is nothing especially humble about them. The name comes from the humming sound they make in flight. They are energetic hard-working, creatures. They visit flowers in search of nectar and pollen, and make wax and honey in much the way honeybees do.

Many bumblebees are handsome and large. In fact the size of a bumblebee's body is so great compared with its wingspread, you may wonder how it can manage to fly. According to the natural laws of flight, bumblebees should not be able to; but fly they do. An anonymous poet once wrote:

I like the joke on the bumble-bee;
His wings are too small to hold him,
He really can't fly, professors agree —
But nobody ever told him.

There are two important differences between the living habits of bumblebees and honeybees. Bumblebees do not make their nests in trees as honeybees do. They nest in the ground or on it, often using the abandoned nests of meadow mice or chipmunks. Overgrown gardens and banks in the earth are also favorite places.

A second difference between the two kinds of bee is the length of a colony's life. In regions where winters are cold, a bumblebee colony dies out at the end of autumn. Only a young queen survives. Honeybee colonies can live through the cold, and may exist for many years.

Spring warmth brings a young bumblebee queen out from her winter resting place. There is no mating flight, for she has already mated with a drone before the winter began. She basks for a while in the sunshine, and looks for food in the newly opening flowers. During the night she seeks shelter, perhaps in the ground or under old leaves. If there is an unseasonable chill, she remains hidden there during the day as well.

After a few weeks the queen is ready to start a new colony. First she must find a site. She makes a careful search of her territory, flying low over the ground. From time to time, she lands to take a closer look. Her choice is not made hurriedly. She may spend days — even weeks — in looking.

Once the queen has found her nest, she makes a tunnel into its center, then burrows out a round chamber. When this is about an inch across, she moves in, keeping the finest of the nesting material close about her. Now and then she crawls outside to find food. She also brings back nectar which she deposits in the nesting material.

Before long the busy queen begins to produce wax, which she uses to build an egg cell. When it is ready, she goes foraging again but now she is searching for pollen. She thrusts this into her egg cell, smooths it carefully, then goes to collect

Bumblebees at the entrances of their underground nests

more. By the time the cell is well stocked, she is ready to lay her first batch of eggs — usually between eight and fourteen. Then she covers the cell with wax and is ready for a new task — the construction of a honeypot. This is finished in a day or two. It is used to store a supply of honey so that when the weather is bad the queen can stay inside her nest.

Bumblebees' honey is like that of the honeybees because it is made from the sweet nectar of flowers. However bumblebees do not convert the sugar in the same way that honeybees do, and the result is not so tasty.

When the tiny bumblebee eggs hatch, the maggot-like larvae start to feed on their bed of pollen. Soon their mother brings them fresh pollen and honey. She feeds them through a break in the wall of each cell. Later she seals the break.

The larvae grow quickly, and each spins a cocoon of silk around itself. Until they emerge as adult bees they need no more to eat.

Inside a bumblebee's nest. The closed cells in the middle contain eggs or larvae. The small, light cells on the right are cocoons. The cells on the left are honeypots.

The wax which had covered the larvae does not go to waste, for the queen uses it to make more egg cells. She is now truly busy — collecting nectar and pollen, building, and incubating her brood with the heat of her body. As the young bees prepare to leave their cocoons, she often helps them to cut through their wrappings.

The first young bees to emerge are all workers. In a few days they are ready to help their queen mother. But although her colony is now well started, she does not become merely an egg-laying machine as honeybee queens do. She continues to feed new broods and carry on other tasks throughout her life.

Bumblebees feed their larvae only honey and pollen. They do not make the bee-bread used by honeybees.

Once a colony is well established with numerous workers, the males and queens are hatched. The young queens help with the chores; the male drones do nothing but eat. Many drones leave the nest quite soon, perhaps not to return again. They forage for their own food and lead independent lives. But before the summer is over they perform their only task. They mate with the queens — either from their own colony or from some other.

As summer progresses, the queen lays fewer and fewer eggs. At last she stops. Then the workers, the old queen, and the drones die. The colony is no more. But young queens, hunting snug retreats in which to spend the winter, give promise of new colonies to come.

actual size

VI
Solitary Bees

Sometime you may see a large black bee busily collecting nectar, and think that it is just another bumblebee. But if you could watch her zoom to her nest, you would find something quite different. There is no waiting colony, only a round tunnel bored into a piece of wood. This bee is one of the solitary group — a "carpenter."

A carpenter bee uses her strong jaws to bore into hard wood. Week after week, almost without rest, she works to cut out a tunnel a foot or more in length. She can bite out only a tiny piece at a time.

When she is finished, the carpenter starts to collect nectar and pollen. She carries this to the end of the tunnel. There she forms it into a cake, on top of which she lays an egg. Then she makes a partition of resin and wood shavings, leaving enough room for the larva to grow when it hatches. She does the same thing over and over again: another cake of nectar and pollen, another egg, another partition. When the tunnel is filled and the entrance closed with a final layer of resin, she flies away for the last time. The young will develop, find a food supply in the nectar-pollen cakes and emerge as adults without further help.

When the young adults burrow their way out of the tunnel, the females and males soon mate. Before long the males die while the females begin the solitary life — each making her own nests and creating new broods.

Closely related to the carpenters is the leaf-cutting bee. It, also, makes tunnels in wood, but usually in rotting timber instead of hard wood. The leaf cutter busies herself snipping oval pieces from leaves — often those of rose bushes. She folds

Large carpenter bee,

actual size

Leaf-cutting bee. It does not have a pollen-basket but carries pollen on the stiff hairs of its abdomen.

each little piece and carries it to her tunnel. When several have been gathered, she rolls them into a thimble-shaped cradle and pushes it to the end of the tunnel. Then she adds a nectar-pollen cake. All is ready for an egg to be laid.

The leaf-cutting bee is small and dainty compared with the larger carpenter bees. Some carpenter bees are very small. They make their homes in the stems of shrubs and flowers rather than in trees. Other species in the tropics bore holes more than an inch in diameter and make tunnels nearly a yard long — in really hard wood.

One of the most amazing of solitary nests is made by one of the mason bees. The female hunts for an empty snail shell in which to deposit a food cake and a single egg. She then makes a cover of chewed leaves, and adds a roof of grass, twigs or pine needles to camouflage it.

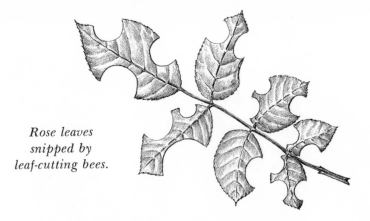

Rose leaves snipped by leaf-cutting bees.

Mason bees build nests in many different places. Some build on a small stone, or against the wall of a building or cliff. Some burrow into clay or sand banks. They cement the inside of the tunnel with a secretion from their bodies to stop the walls from falling in.

Because some solitary bees nest close together, in great numbers, they appear to live like social bees. However, they do not work together as a colony does. They gather together because the site has the right conditions for them — open ground with good drainage or the plants and trees they need for their tunnels. Each bee fends for herself and takes no notice of her neighbors unless the whole group is threatened. Then the insects fly at the intruder in a united and infuriated swarm.

When an area is riddled with the nests of many solitary bees, it is known as a bee town. There is one such "town" in Utah made up of something like *two hundred thousand* individual nesting sites.

Leaf-cutter nests. Left, a nest made of bits of leaves, built in the ground. The opened cells show an egg and a larva with their food supplies.

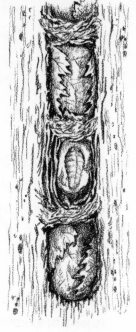

Right, a nest built in wood.

Mason bee nests, made of small pieces of stone glued toge[r]

Small carpenter bee nest in the pith of a twig, showing young and food supply

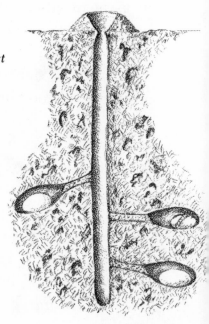

Entrances of mining bee nests in a dirt bank

Cross-section of one type of mining bee nest, showing youn[g] and food supply

VII
Stingless Bees

What kind of bee does not have a sting? It might be a drone, because a male does not have a sting. But it could also be one of a large group of "stingless" bees.

Stingless bees live in the warmer parts of the world — in South America and Mexico and in some areas on the other side of the world. There are several hundred species. All of them are small compared with honeybees. The smallest measures about one-twelfth of an inch; the largest is less than three-eighths of an inch.

Tiny as they are, the stingless bees are great workers. Members of a colony produce honey and wax, and they build remarkable nests. Some of them spend much time collecting clay, which they build into barricades around the nest as a protection against possible enemies. They are masons as well as pollen gatherers and workers in wax.

Although different kinds of stingless bees make

different kinds of homes, they follow one general plan. The nest is divided into two chambers — one for the brood of young, the other for storing honey and pollen. The horizontal combs of wax which they construct are supported one above the other by tiny pillars. Between the combs there are occasional gaps through which nurse bees can pass as they take care of the young.

Some Australian stingless bees make their combs in the shape of an irregular spiral staircase. Each comb, encased in wax, winds upward, tapering toward the end.

Some stingless bees make no regular combs. They simply heap their cells in clusters.

A colony of stingless bees is made up of three types of members — queen, workers and drones — as is a colony of honeybees. But the drones seem to take an active part in domestic life. They help to clean the nest and raise the young bees.

The nests house enormous numbers of bees. They also hold large amounts of honey. The largest nests of the Australian stingless bee have been known to yield as much as fifty pounds about twice a year. In South America, the Indians of the Amazon Valley can take as much as two quarts from a nest of average size. In Mexico the Maya Indians began to domesticate stingless bees hundreds of years ago. They housed the bees in hollow logs.

Recently an explorer lost in the dense wilderness along the Amazon River came upon a colony of stingless bees in an old termite nest. In a few minutes he cut through to the honey with his bush knife. Using a leaf as a spoon, he managed to get some to his mouth in spite of the furious bees hovering around him. Though the honey was not the best grade, it saved his life by quenching his thirst and hunger for a short time.

Usually, however, explorers are warned against eating the honey of wild stingless bees. These insects do not always choose flowers from which to collect food. Some may feed on the remains of dead animals and other refuse. As a result their honey can be poisonous to humans.

Although these bees are called "stingless," this is not a strictly correct description. They still have

Stingless bee

actual size

the remains of stinging equipment. When they attack an enemy, they go through the motions of stinging. Probably many ages ago they could really sting, but their weapon no longer works. They cannot inflict a wound with it.

The stingless bees are far from defenseless, however. Their bite is quite ferocious, and when a number of them set upon a victim, they can inflict real pain. The smallest of them can cause even more misery than the larger varieties. They crawl into a person's ears, nostrils, hair and eyes. In Brazil a common name for very tiny stingless bees is "eye-lickers."

VIII
They All Like Honey

Honey tastes good — not only to people, but to a number of animals. Many small creatures, such as field mice, enjoy it. A number of insects such as ants, wasps, and certain moths like it also. However, the amounts they take are too small to matter to the bees.

Bears are particularly fond of honey. One of the earliest lessons a bear cub learns is how to rob a bee tree. His mother teaches him to lick the sweet syrup out of a hive with his tongue. The bear still has to pay for the honey. Although a heavy coat protects much of his body, the soft skin around the nose can be badly hurt. And that is where the bees attack with their poison daggers.

Bears like to raid bee nests. They eat both honey and grubs.

Long ago, great forests covered most of Europe. They sheltered many swarms of honeybees; they also sheltered bears. Had the bees not been able to defend their homes from the big, shaggy robbers with their stings, they would not have survived. In a matter of seconds, a bear could strip a colony of the honey stored by the bees through many long days' work.

Man gradually took over the land, and wild mammals — including bears — grew scarce. But people became an even greater threat to bees than the bears had been. Men could empty hives with very little trouble. They helped themselves to the bees' treasure with no thought for the future. Finally man began to realize he was wiping out the insects that made the delicious honey. He began to use more care. He no longer destroyed nests, but left enough honey so that bees would have food for their own needs.

One of the strangest hive robbers is an African forest bird known as the honey guide. It is a small brownish-gray bird and it has no means, such as a strong beak, of breaking into hives. It has keen eyesight, however, and flies many miles a day on the lookout for bee colonies.

Honey guide

Honey badger, or ratel

When the honey guide finds a colony, it goes off to look for a partner. Very often the partner is a shaggy, short-legged animal called a honey badger. The bird flies close to him, chattering excitedly. When it catches the badger's attention, it leads him to the honey.

The two partners reach the bee colony, and the bird perches on a nearby tree while the badger sets to work. He climbs to the nest, and rips away the wood with his sharp, strong claws. Although the furious insects may be buzzing around and stinging him, he is not greatly bothered. His coarse, heavy fur and tough hide give him protection.

Once the honey is uncovered, the badger has a feast. He takes no notice of the honey guide. The bird waits patiently. It knows there will be something left for it. Actually, the bird likes the larvae and their wax brood cells even better than the honey. When bird and badger have finished, there is very little left of a hive.

Sometimes a honey guide looks for a man who lives in the forest. Man and bird keep track of each other by whistling and chattering as they go toward the beehive. Of course the man could easily remove every bit of the honey for himself, but as a rule people treat the honey guide fairly. They take care to leave some "pickings." Today few African natives depend on the honey guide; they make beehives and place them in trees near their homes.

IX
Bees and Men

Men have kept bees for thousands of years. People of the Stone Age knew the value of honey as food. At first they doubtless stole it from hives of wild bees. Then they learned to make crude hives from hollow logs, placing sticks in them to support honey combs. Finally, European farmers invented a kind of upside-down basket called a skep, which became popular as a beehive.

By the Middle Ages bees had won high regard as producers of honey. A painting made more than four hundred years ago by the Italian artist Piero Di Cosimo shows honey being discovered in a gnarled, twisted tree by smiling mythical characters.

In more recent years honey has become the basis of a great industry. In the United States alone there are more than five million hives, and hundreds of millions of pounds of honey are sold each year.

Today, farmers also keep bees for the good of

their crops. Pollen from the flowers has to be placed on waiting pistils so that seeds will form. Sometimes the wind carries the pollen from one blossom to another. But often it is carried by insects such as flies, butterflies, moths, beetles, wasps — and bees.

Many years ago, bees were valued only because of the honey they produced. Little thought was given to their value in carrying pollen. However, as the forests disappeared and wild bees became more and more scarce, farmers began to realize how helpful these insects were to agriculture. Now great numbers of hive bees are kept simply to pollinize flowers.

Straw hives, called skeps, are often used in Europe

Modern wooden hive. At the bottom is a brood chamber, shown open, and, above it, a storage chamber

For successful pollination, the pollen taken from one plant must reach the flowers of other plants of the same species. This happens regularly because certain species of bee specialize in the flowers they visit. For the most part, when a bee is collecting nectar, it always stops at the same kind of flower.

The bumblebee is particularly interested in red clover. Its very long tongue allows it to reach the nectar at the end of the long corolla tubes. When farmers in New Zealand first tried to grow clover, they were not successful. Though they planted field after field, few seeds resulted. Then several species of bumblebees were brought into the country. Soon the seed production increased.

Farmers could count on continuing crops. Honey-bees carry pollen for at least fifty plants on which people depend, particularly alfalfa and fruit trees. In some areas "leaf-cutting" bees help to pollinate alfalfa. They also carry pollen for buckwheat and clover, marigolds and morning-glories.

Despite all that men have learned about keeping bees for profit, unexpected problems still arise This is a recent one. For many years in Brazil, hives of Italian honeybees and German honeybees were the outstanding producers. They were gentle and easy to manage. Then someone in the industry decided to bring bees from Africa into his colonies. These were quite ferocious, but they produced thirty per cent more honey than honeybees of other countries.

Twenty queens were taken from Africa to Brazil and, as had been expected, a crossbreed re-

In a garden in Iran, hollow logs serve as bee-hives

More than 300 years before Christ, the Greeks of Ephesus used the honeybee as a design on one of their coins

sulted. But, unexpectedly, the new breed of bees was even more ferocious than its African ancestors. The bees attacked not only people and farm animals, they turned on other bees, killing off hive after hive.

The terrible-tempered bees were able to live in all kinds of places — in caves, under rocks and tree roots, in telephone booths and on traffic lights. Generation after generation continued to be strong, bold and vicious. Although the original African queens were destroyed, the damage had been done. Brazilian beekeepers are still trying to undo the serious trouble they created.

Happily, anything of this sort is very unusual. If the African bees — known to be ferocious — had not been taken from their natural surroundings, the problem would not have been created.

Left undisturbed, bees are inclined to lead their busy lives quite peacefully. Year after year, they carry pollen for flowers without assistance from anyone. Year after year, they produce valuable honey for themselves and for people. Man is fortunate to have so many of these insects working for him because they are thoroughly independent. Yet when Man the Beekeeper makes living conditions convenient and comfortable for his honey-makers, he is usually well repaid.

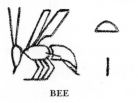

BEE

HONEY

The ancient Egyptians gathered honey from wild bees, kept bees in their gardens, and even used a bee in their hieroglyphs, or sign-writing (left). Because they thought so highly of the bee, they used the same sign to mean "King of Upper and Lower Egypt." Below, in hieroglyphs, is the name of one of the great kings who ruled in the 15th Century B.C.

KING OF UPPER AND LOWER EGYPT \   THUTMOSIS

APPENDIX

Bees in the Animal Kingdom

All members of the great animal kingdom are related, just by being animals. But many closer relationships may be noted. There are animals with backbones (the vertebrates) more closely related to each other than they are to animals without backbones (the invertebrates). Among the various groups of invertebrates are the anthropods, all members of which have jointed legs. Such a group is known as a phylum. The anthropods are, in turn, divided into classes. One of these is made up of insects.

The insects, too, have their divisions, or orders. One of the orders is called Hymenoptera. Among its more important members are ants, wasps — and bees.

In the bee group are divisions — the families, made up of honeybees, bumblebees, stingless bees, and solitary bees; and within these family groups are divisions of genus and species. The entire bee group is named Apoidea.

About insects: All, in their adult form, have six legs. The body of every insect is made up of three parts — head, thorax, and abdomen. Antennae

56

(most insects have them) are attached to the head. Wings and legs are attached to the thorax. Insects do not have an internal skeleton but have a hard covering about their bodies called chitin.

BEE FAMILIES *and some of their divisions*

Family COLLETIDAE

One genus: *Colletes* (colletid bees)
One species: *Colletes compactus* [found east of the Rocky Mountains]

Family ANDRENIDAE

One genus: *Andrena* (mining bees)
One species: *Andrena carlini* [found east of the Rocky Mountains]

Family HALICTIDAE

One genus: *Halictus* (sweat bees)
One species: *Halictus farinosus* [found from New Mexico to California; north to Montana and British Columbia]

Family MEGACHILIDAE

One genus: *Megachile* (leafcutting bees)
One species: *Megachile latimanus* [found east of the Rocky Mountains]

Family APIDAE

Genus: *Xylocopa* (carpenter bees)
One species: *Xylocopa virginica* [found in eastern and southern North America]
Genus: *Bombus* (bumblebees)
One species: *Bombus americanorum* [found throughout the United States and southern Canada]
Genus: *Apis* (honeybees)
One species: *Apis mellifera* [found throughout much of North America; imported from Europe]

Family MELIPONIDAE

Genus: *Melipona* (stingless bees)
One species: *Melipona beecheii* [found in Mexico and Central America]

Index

Italic page numbers indicate illustrations

Honey Guide, 47, *47*, 48, 49
Honeybees, *2*, *3*, *4*, *9*, 12, 13, *14*, 15, 16, *16*, 17, *17*,
    18, *18*, 20, *20*, 21, *21*, 22, *22*, 23, *23*, *24*, 25, 26, *26*,
    27, *27*, 28, *28*, 29-31, 33, 41, 42, 46, 53, *54*, *55*, 57
    African, 53, 54
    Drones, *6*, 15-17, *17*, 18, 41
    German, 53
    Italian, 53
    Queens, 9, 15, 16, *16*, 17, 18, *18*, 19, *19*, 20, 22, 23,
        27, 34, 53, 54
    Workers, *2*, *3*, *4*, 7, 15, 16, *16*, 17, *17*, 18, 20, *20*, *21*,
        22, *22*, 23, *23*, 25
    See also Hives, Honeycombs.
Honeycombs, *14-15*, 17, 18, *18*, 21, 26, *26*, 27, 29, 42,
    50
    Brood Cells, 16, *18*, 20-22, 42, 49, 52, *52*
    Queen Cells, 17, 18, *18*, 19, *19*
    Storage Cells, *14-15*, 15, *18*, *21-23*, 42, 52, *52*
Honeypot, 33, *33*
Hymenoptera, 57

Indians, 29, 42
Iran, 53

Language. *See* Bee Dances
Larvae, 17, 18, *18*, 33, *33*, 34, 36, *40*, 46, 49
Leaf-cutting Bee, 37, 38, *38*, *40*, 53
    Tunnels of, 37, *40*

Mandibles, *4*, 7, 36
Mason Bees, 38, *40*
    Cement of, 39, 40
    Nests of, 38, 39, *40*
Mating. *See* Bees.
Mating Flight, 15, 17, 19, 31
Mexico, 41, 42
Middle Ages, 59
Mining Bee, *40*
    Nests of, *40*

Dorothy E. Shuttlesworth brings to this book her long experience as a writer of natural history.

After editing Junior Natural History Magazine for twelve years she turned to writing full-time. She has provided bulletins for the National Audubon Society and has written fourteen books for boys and girls.

Dorothy Shuttlesworth now lives in East Orange, New Jersey with her husband and two children.

Su Zan Noguchi Swain was born in Iliff, Colorado, and holds degrees from the Universities of Colorado and Pennsylvania. She now lives in Chatham, New Jersey with her two sons. An illustrator since 1938, she has a long list of titles to her credit. ALL KINDS OF BEES is her fourth collaboration with Dorothy Shuttlesworth. In 1953, she received the unique distinction of being made an Honorary Life Member of the New York Entomological Society for "consistently excellent drawings and paintings of insects and other natural history subjects".